The Proverbs 31-ish Woman

Snarky Truths and Grace-Filled Grit for Women Figuring Out Faith One Flawed Day at a Time

By Diane Ferreira

Published by:

Vale & Vine Press – Vale & Vine Books

Cromwell, Connecticut

ISBN: 979-8-9993872-3-3

Library of Congress Control Number: 2025942537

Cover and interior design by Diane Ferreira.

Printed in the United States of America.

To the women holding it together with dry shampoo, duct tape, and divine strength. This one's for you.

Acknowledgments

To Jesus…because without You, I'd be a hot mess with no message.

To my family, who let me write while the laundry exploded. And to my friends, who read every chapter and said, "Girl, you better."

To every woman who's ever wondered if she's enough: you are, and then some. Keep showing up. Keep laughing. Keep rising.

Table of Contents

THE PROVERBS 31-ISH WOMAN

INTRODUCTION: THE PROVERBS 31-ISH WOMAN

CHAPTER 1: SHE RISES WHILE IT'S STILL NIGHT (BECAUSE SHE HAS TO PEE)

CHAPTER 2: SHE IS CLOTHED IN STRENGTH AND DIGNITY (AND SOMETIMES THAT HOODIE FROM 2008)

CHAPTER 3: SHE WATCHES OVER THE AFFAIRS OF HER HOUSEHOLD (WHILE GOOGLING 'HOW TO DISAPPEAR INTO THE WOODS')

CHAPTER 4: SHE OPENS HER MOUTH WITH WISDOM (RIGHT AFTER SAYING SOMETHING SHE SHOULDN'T HAVE)

CHAPTER 5: SHE GIRDS HERSELF WITH STRENGTH (BECAUSE LIFE KEEPS TRYING HER)

CHAPTER 6: SHE CONSIDERS A FIELD AND BUYS IT (OR ADDS IT TO HER CART AND ABANDONS IT BY NOON)

CHAPTER 7: HER HUSBAND PRAISES HER (BUT STILL CAN'T FIND THE KETCHUP)

CHAPTER 8: SHE LAUGHS AT THE DAYS TO COME (BECAUSE SHE'S ALREADY CRIED ABOUT THEM)

CHAPTER 9: HER CHILDREN RISE UP AND CALL HER BLESSED (AFTER THEY ASK WHAT'S FOR DINNER)

CHAPTER 10: SHE DOES HIM GOOD, NOT HARM (EVEN WHEN HE FORGETS TRASH DAY AGAIN)

CHAPTER 11: SHE WORKS WITH WILLING HANDS (AND SLIGHTLY BITTER COMMENTARY)

CHAPTER 12: SHE IS NOT AFRAID OF SNOW FOR HER HOUSEHOLD (BECAUSE SHE'S STOCKED THE SNACKS AND PRAYED OVER THE PIPES)

CHAPTER 13: SHE BRINGS HER FOOD FROM AFAR (AKA: SHE KNOWS THE DOORDASH GUY BY NAME)

CHAPTER 14: SHE MAKES LINEN GARMENTS AND SELLS THEM (OR JUST OPENED AN ETSY SHOP AND CAN'T FIND HER TAPE GUN)

CHAPTER 15: STRENGTH AND HONOR ARE HER CLOTHING (BUT ALSO LEGGINGS AND THAT ONE SWEATSHIRT SHE'S HAD SINCE 2009)

CHAPTER 16: HER LAMP DOES NOT GO OUT AT NIGHT (BECAUSE SHE'S DOOMSCROLLING AT 1AM)

CHAPTER 18: SHE FEARS THE LORD... AND RUNNING INTO SOMEONE SHE WENT TO HIGH SCHOOL WITH

CHAPTER 19: CHARM IS DECEPTIVE, BEAUTY IS FLEETING, AND INSTAGRAM IS A LIE

THE PROVERBS 31-ISH WOMAN RISES AGAIN (WITH COFFEE, CHRIST, AND A HAIR TIE ON HER WRIST)

ABOUT THE AUTHOR

INTRODUCTION: The Proverbs 31-ish Woman

Let me just go ahead and say it: Proverbs 31 has haunted more women than low-rise jeans and middle school dances combined. You know the one. That virtuous woman with her flax, her fields, her flawless morning routine; the original Pinterest mom with no under-eye bags and a fully stocked pantry.

Meanwhile, the rest of us are just trying to figure out if coffee counts as breakfast and whether yelling "I'm fine!" through gritted teeth counts as emotional regulation.

This book is not for the woman who has it all together. This is for the rest of us. The ones who love Jesus but occasionally lose it in traffic. The ones who believe in grace but also believe that leggings can be pants. The ones who want to be virtuous but also want to be left alone with carbs and Christian radio.

I am a Proverbs 31-ish woman.

I'm up while it is still night, yes...because I have insomnia and the dog won't stop licking his toes. I consider a field, sure, but usually while scrolling Zillow for houses I'll never buy. I open my mouth with wisdom, occasionally, right after I say something petty and then repent immediately.

This "ish" is holy.

And I believe with my whole heart that God is not waiting for us to be perfect before He uses us. I believe He meets us right in the messy, hormonal, hilarious, hot-mess middle and says, "Yes, daughter. That part. Let's work with *that*."

So, in these pages, you're going to laugh. You're going to feel seen. And you might even snort coffee out your nose (which, let's be honest, is the true sign of anointing).

We're taking Proverbs 31 out of the glass case and putting her right in the carpool lane. We're making room for her to be real, to be relatable, and yes, to be funny. Because holiness doesn't mean humorless. And virtue doesn't mean vanilla.

You ready, sis?

Let's redefine the virtuous woman, one slightly sarcastic, deeply sacred, snack-filled chapter at a time.

Pass the snacks. Grab your Bible. And let's do this.

CHAPTER 1: She Rises While It's Still Night (Because She Has to Pee)

Let's be honest. If "rising while it is still night" was a spiritual badge of honor, then congratulations to every perimenopausal woman out there. We are elite. We are chosen. We are up at 2:47 a.m. for no apparent reason other than our bladder and a brain that thinks now is a good time to rehash that awkward text we sent in 2013.

Now listen, I know Proverbs 31:15 is supposed to inspire us with the image of this majestic woman waking before dawn to prepare food for her household. That's beautiful. But I'm just trying to make it to the coffee pot without stubbing my toe and yelling a word that rhymes with "spit."

I do rise while it is still night. But not for noble reasons. I rise because my body has the circadian rhythm of a haunted Roomba. I rise because I'm sweating, my pillow betrayed me, and my dog thinks 3 a.m. is prime time for changing position 15 times and licking his feet.

But here's the thing. Those quiet hours before the sun comes up? They can be sacred too. It's in those pajama-clad, eye-crusty moments that some of the rawest, realest conversations with God happen. Not because we're spiritual superheroes. But because we are too tired to fake it.

There's no performance at 3 a.m. There's no pretending to be Pinterest-perfect. It's just us, God, and the creaky floorboards. That's where He meets us. In the messy middle of motherhood, ministry, and midlife madness.

So no, I may not be baking bread at dawn. But I am learning to bless the broken sleep. I'm learning to stop resenting the wake-ups and start welcoming the whispers of God that come when the world is still and the Wi-Fi is quiet.

And if nothing else, I now know where every squeaky floorboard is in my house. That has to count for something.

So, the next time you find yourself awake while the world sleeps, just remember you're not alone. The Proverbs 31-ish woman is up too, probably Googling "natural remedies for night sweats" while asking God to calm her brain and bless her caffeine.

Amen and good morning.

CHAPTER 2: *She is Clothed in Strength and Dignity (And Sometimes That Hoodie From 2008)*

Let's just be clear: strength and dignity are not mutually exclusive with stretch pants and a messy bun. I checked. It's not in the Bible.

Yes, Proverbs 31 says she is clothed in strength and dignity, and I believe it. But I also believe she probably had a favorite robe that was one spilled cup of goat milk away from being retired.

Dignity isn't about pearls and posture. It's about showing up anyway. It's about holding your head high even when your roots are showing and your last good bra gave up the ghost. It's being the woman who walks into a room with spiritual authority, even if she's also carrying three grocery bags on one arm and a rogue Cheerio stuck to her sock.

We have been taught that dignity looks like poise, polish, and perfect edges. But what if dignity looks more like endurance? Like rising up again after falling on your face. Like answering emails while crying into your laundry pile. Like biting your tongue when someone absolutely deserves a well-placed scripture to the forehead. It's not about never breaking…it's about not staying broken.

Strength? Baby, strength is not a six-pack and a green smoothie habit. Strength is showing up to the meeting when your soul wants to crawl back under the covers. Strength is forgiving someone for the ninth time and still choosing not to tell everyone what they did.

Strength is saying yes to God when your whole flesh is screaming "absolutely not." Strength is looking in the mirror, seeing the messy, vulnerable version of yourself, and choosing to love her anyway.

You want to talk strength? Let's talk about the woman who shows up to her life, even when it doesn't look like she thought it would. The one who walks into church with mascara from Tuesday and a smile that says, "God's not finished with me yet." The one who holds onto her faith like it's a lifeline, even when the waves of doubt, depression, or dirty dishes threaten to pull her under.

And you know what else? Strength is also knowing when to rest. It's trusting that God is still moving even when you're sitting your tired behind down with a blanket, a show, and a snack. Rest is holy. Sabbath isn't weakness, it's wisdom.

So maybe today you're not feeling very strong. Maybe your dignity feels like it's being held together with dry shampoo and coffee. But don't let that lie get louder than the truth: you are clothed in strength and dignity; not because you feel it, but because God said it. And He doesn't change His mind based on your mood or your laundry pile.

And that hoodie from 2008? It's holy now. Don't let anyone tell you otherwise. Wrap yourself in it, wear it like a blessing, and walk into your calling with your head held high and maybe a snack in your pocket.

You, my friend, are the real deal.

CHAPTER 3: She Watches Over the Affairs of Her Household (While Googling 'How to Disappear Into the Woods')

Now let's talk about one of the greatest lies we tell ourselves: that running a household is just "keeping the house clean." Sis. No.

Watching over the affairs of your household is not about the dishes in the sink, it's about the chaos in the group text, the emotional temperature of your teenager, the whereabouts of your spouse's favorite hoodie (which you secretly stole), and whether anyone remembered to defrost the chicken.

When Proverbs 31 says she watches over the affairs of her household, I'm convinced this woman had next-level intuition, a rotating meal plan, and the Holy Spirit whispering reminders in her ear like, "Don't forget it's pajama day at school."

The mental load? She carried it before it was a hashtag. She wasn't just running a home. She was running a *life system*. Logistics, schedules, conflict resolution, prayer covering, Amazon returns, spiritual guidance, and remembering everyone's allergies.

And let's be honest, sometimes it's just a little too much. Sometimes you want to throw your phone into a drawer, slap a "Do Not Disturb Unless Someone Is On Fire" sign on your forehead, and escape to a cabin where no one asks what's for dinner.

But here's the beauty: God doesn't expect perfection in your household. He's looking for presence. For attentiveness. For that heart that says, "Lord, help me do this with grace and a decent Wi-Fi signal."

Because watching over your household isn't about control, it's about stewardship. It's about being the spiritual thermostat when everyone else is throwing emotional bombs. It's about seeing the big picture when everyone else is hyper focused on their cereal not being the right kind.

You're not "just" a mom or "just" a wife or "just" anything. You are the command center of your family's daily rhythm. And even when you feel invisible, your impact is undeniable.

So, keep watching. Keep praying. Keep showing up. Even if your version of "watching over" includes Netflix in one eye and a to-do list in the other.

You're doing holy work. And that's worth everything.

CHAPTER 4: *She Opens Her Mouth With Wisdom (Right After Saying Something She Shouldn't Have)*

Look, we all *want* to be the wise woman whose words drip with grace and gentle conviction. But sometimes? Sometimes that wisdom doesn't kick in until approximately 4.7 seconds after we've already said the thing we'll be repenting for.

"She opens her mouth with wisdom." Yes, Lord, we love that verse. We write it on mugs. We post it on social media. But let's be honest, some days it feels more like: "She opens her mouth and deeply regrets it later."

It's not that we *don't* have wisdom. It's just that sometimes our sarcasm gets there first. Sometimes our tone decides to go rogue. Sometimes the filter malfunctions and the Holy Spirit has to hit us with that gentle nudge: "Daughter... was *that* necessary?"

And that's where grace steps in. Because the Proverbs 31-ish woman isn't perfect, she's growing. She learns when to speak and when to sip her tea and mind her business. She's figuring out that wisdom doesn't always need a microphone. Sometimes it needs a muzzle. Or a mute button. Or a snack.

Wisdom knows that not every group chat deserves a reply (really...do we even need a group chat at all??). Not every family drama requires your intervention. Not every petty post on Facebook needs your "righteous" comment typed in all caps.

Wisdom is discerning when to bring the truth and when to bring tacos. When to quote scripture and when to quietly pray from the passenger seat while gripping the dashboard.

Opening your mouth with wisdom doesn't mean you never mess up. It means you're learning to slow down, check your motives, and let the Holy Spirit have the mic more than your flesh does.

And let's be real…sometimes wisdom sounds like, "I'm sorry."

Sometimes it looks like deleting the paragraph you *really* wanted to post. Sometimes it means letting people be wrong on the internet because your peace is more precious than being right.

So go ahead, sis. Keep growing in grace. Keep choosing better words. But don't beat yourself up when you miss it. Just own it, learn from it, and maybe keep a few breath mints on hand for the next round.

Because the Proverbs 31-ish woman? She's learning to open her mouth with wisdom, even if she has to put her foot in it first.

CHAPTER 5: She Girds Herself with Strength (Because Life Keeps Trying Her)

Let's talk about girding, shall we? First of all, "gird" is one of those biblical words that sounds vaguely uncomfortable. Like something involving Spanx and regret.

But in Proverbs 31, when it says she "girds herself with strength," it's not just about physical stamina. It's about being spiritually strapped in because life is out here throwing emotional dodgeballs.

This woman isn't lifting weights, she's lifting expectations, lifting family drama, lifting everyone else's junk off the floor (literal and emotional). And she doesn't even get a trophy. She gets eye bags and the occasional back spasm.

Strength, in her case, looks like resilience. Like walking through the fire without smelling like smoke. Like praying for her kids while also Googling "how to not scream at your loved ones." Like holding it together with one hand while heating up leftovers with the other and somehow still remembering the Wi-Fi password.

You know what this world doesn't see? The quiet strength it takes to stay married when everything in you wants to peace out and go live with the sea turtles. The holy grit it takes to show up to church after a week from the pits of Hades and still lift your hands during worship without slapping anyone in your row.

She girds herself because strength is not handed to her, it's chosen. She chooses to get up again. She chooses to forgive. She chooses to be kind when her mouth wants to say something that would need to be bleeped out of a Sunday sermon.

And you know what else? She doesn't always feel strong. But strength isn't a feeling. It's a decision. It's a mindset. It's trusting that God's power is made perfect in weakness, so her weakness is not the disqualifier, it's the invitation.

So, if today you feel stretched thin, worn down, or just plain tired of trying, hear this: strength doesn't mean you're unfazed. It means you haven't quit.

Gird yourself, sis. With scripture, with grace, with the last ounce of humor you've got in the tank. The world may keep trying you, but the Holy Spirit is training you. And you? You're stronger than you think.

CHAPTER 6: She Considers a Field and Buys It (Or Adds It to Her Cart and Abandons It by Noon)

Now this is where the Proverbs 31 woman gets business-savvy. She considers a field and buys it. She's out here evaluating property like a boss. Meanwhile, you and I are staring at a grocery app wondering if we really need avocados or if that's just the devil tempting us with guac-based disappointment.

This woman isn't impulsive. She's intentional. She looks at the field. She thinks about the value. She weighs the cost. She's not just tossing money around like it's Monopoly and the Lord's her banker. She's strategic. She sees purpose before purchase.

Now, before you start comparing your Amazon cart full of decorative throw pillows to her real estate portfolio, take a deep breath. Because the field isn't always literal. Sometimes the field is a calling. A relationship. A dream you've been too scared to pursue.

When you "consider a field," you're looking at something that could grow. Could bear fruit. Could be a place where God plants you and says, "Tend this."

And yes, sometimes you walk away. Because not every opportunity is your assignment. Some things look fruitful but are just distractions dressed in potential. The Proverbs 31-ish woman knows that just because something is shiny doesn't mean it's sanctified.

But when she *does* buy it? Whew. Watch out. She invests. She builds. She turns that field into a harvest. Not because she had it all figured out, but because she trusted the process. Because she moved when God said move.

So maybe your "field" isn't land. Maybe it's that book you've been too scared to write. The class you've been meaning to take. The ministry God put on your heart that feels too big for your current bandwidth. My friend, consider it. Pray on it. Then get to buying. Buy into the dream. Buy into the work. Then dig your heels in and cultivate the life God dared you to imagine while the dryer buzzed and dinner burned.

Don't overthink it. Don't stall out. The field is waiting. And girl, you were born to grow something holy.

CHAPTER 7: Her Husband Praises Her (But Still Can't Find the Ketchup)

Let's have a moment of holy honesty: being praised by your husband is wonderful. It's uplifting, affirming, and occasionally suspicious. Like, "What do you want and how expensive is it?"

Proverbs 31 says her husband rises and calls her blessed. And girl, we love that for her. We do. But it also says nothing about whether he puts his laundry in the basket or remembers your birthday without a calendar invite.

You can be deeply loved and still mildly irritated. You can be praised and still feel like the house would catch fire if you left for more than 48 hours. That's marriage, baby. It's messy and beautiful, sanctifying and snack-filled, and every now and then it makes you question your life choices while looking for the TV remote he swears he didn't touch.

There's a holy tension in loving someone who is both your biggest fan and your biggest mystery. He can fix a car, negotiate with insurance, and survive a staff meeting with ten grown men, but can't locate the ketchup that is literally on the middle shelf, staring him in the face. This isn't a marriage crisis. This is male pattern blindness, and it's biblical. Probably.

And don't even get me started on praise. Sometimes his version of "praise" is a half-hearted grunt while scrolling through sports highlights. Other times, it's a dramatic proclamation like, "No one makes spaghetti like you," as if you just performed a culinary miracle and didn't just dump a jar of marinara into a pot while praying the noodles don't clump.

But here's the thing. The Proverbs 31-ish woman isn't waiting for praise to validate her worth. She doesn't need applause to know she's doing the thing. Her value isn't rooted in recognition. It's rooted in obedience. In consistency. In walking it out even when no one's clapping.

And when her husband *does* praise her? She receives it with grace. She doesn't deflect with sarcasm (okay, maybe just a little). She doesn't brush it off. Because being seen…truly seen…for your effort, your heart, your faithfulness, that's a gift. Even if it comes with a side of "Have you seen my keys?"

Let's normalize the "both-and" of Christian marriage. You can love your husband and still want to hide in the pantry with a sleeve of cookies. You can serve your family and still fantasize about a solo trip to a hotel where the towels are magically clean and no one calls your name through the door.

Marriage is a ministry. It's a long game. It's choosing to believe the best even when you're certain he's going to leave his socks under the coffee table for the 11th day in a row. It's smiling at him during communion while plotting to rearrange all the cabinets just to see if he notices.

So yes, let him praise you. Let him call you blessed. But whether he notices or not, keep showing up. Keep loving well. Keep leaning into God more than you lean into their validation.

Because you, my dear, are praiseworthy, even if you're the only one in the house who knows where the ketchup is.

CHAPTER 8: *She Laughs at the Days to Come (Because She's Already Cried About Them)*

There's something deeply spiritual about laughing when nothing makes sense. Like a sacred act of defiance. A giggle in the face of chaos. A chuckle through clenched teeth while microwaving chicken nuggets and wondering if adulthood was a trap sent by Satan.

The Proverbs 31 woman laughs at the days to come. Not because she's naive, but because she knows something the rest of us are still figuring out: God's got this. And He's got her. Even when everything feels out of control and her mascara is migrating south.

But let's not romanticize it. This kind of laughter doesn't come from a life of ease. It's not the laugh of someone who has a cleaning schedule and a crockpot that's never betrayed her. It's the laugh of a woman who's seen things.

Who's walked through the fire, stepped on Legos barefoot, and come out the other side with a testimony and a to-go coffee.

She laughs because she's learned that anxiety doesn't change outcomes, but it will absolutely steal your snacks. She laughs because the alternative is screaming into a throw pillow and emotionally adopting a llama.

She laughs because somewhere deep in her spirit, there's a joy that isn't based on circumstances but on the unshakable truth that she's not doing life alone.

Joy isn't denial. It's defiance. It's shouting "Not today, Satan" in Target while holding a clearance candle and an iced chai. It's knowing you have no idea what next week will look like, but you're showing up anyway…mascara running, to-do list half done, and a boldness that smells faintly of dry shampoo and Jesus.

She laughs because she remembers the last time she thought it would all fall apart, and it didn't. Or maybe it *did*, but she survived anyway.

She cried, she prayed, she ordered takeout three nights in a row, and somehow the world kept turning. That kind of history with God gives you a holy kind of humor. The kind that knows the pit isn't permanent and the storm always ends.

This laugh? It's not cute and polite. It's not a giggle tucked behind a teacup. This laugh is loud and ugly and full-bodied...the kind that makes people stare at the grocery store and makes your kids ask, "Are you okay?" It's a laugh rooted in redemption. A laugh that says, "I've been through hell, and I came out with stronger faith and a better eyebrow pencil."

So, when the days ahead look big and messy and wildly unpredictable, laugh anyway. Laugh because the One who holds the future also holds your hand. Laugh because joy is your protest and your praise. Laugh because even in the middle of the mess, there's always something holy growing.

And laugh loud, sis. The devil hates that. And honestly? That's half the fun.

CHAPTER 9: *Her Children Rise Up and Call Her Blessed (After They Ask What's for Dinner)*

You know what's wild? The Bible says her children rise up and call her blessed. Not "tired," not "over it," not "one grocery trip away from snapping." Blessed. Which is a real flex when you think about how often motherhood feels like unpaid Uber driving with a side of mystery laundry.

Kids are a blessing. Yes. Absolutely. But let's not pretend they don't also test every spiritual fruit you've ever claimed to have. You think you're patient until someone spills an entire gallon of milk and looks at you like it was your fault for buying milk in the first place.

Still, the Proverbs 31-ish woman somehow does it. She loves big. She leads well. She knows when to lay hands, and when to lay down the law.

But here's the real magic: she's not waiting for a perfect Hallmark moment to feel validated. Her kids might not always rise up with praise. Sometimes they rise up with attitude and cereal demands. Sometimes their version of "I love you" is a text that says, "we're out of Pop-Tarts."

And yet, she keeps showing up. She shows up with snacks, with scripture, with sanity mostly intact. She shows up when she's exhausted. She shows up when they roll their eyes. She shows up when she'd rather hide in her car listening to worship music and avoiding everyone with her sunglasses and a Diet Coke.

Because that's what love does.

She doesn't need them to be perfect. She just wants them to know they're seen, safe, and scandalously loved. She's not building robots. She's raising world changers. Kids who might one day actually appreciate how she held it together while holding them up.

And when they finally do rise up and call her blessed…whether it's with a hug, a thank-you, or just not slamming the car door for once…she'll receive it with a heart full of grace and maybe a little smug smile.

Because blessed is exactly what she is.

CHAPTER 10: She Does Him Good, Not Harm (Even When He Forgets Trash Day Again)

Let's just pause and give a collective eye roll for every time a husband has walked right past a full trash can like it was an art installation. The Bible says she does him good, not harm, all the days of her life. That includes the days when he forgets to pick up milk, leaves the toilet seat up, or tries to fix something that clearly needs a professional.

Doing him good doesn't mean she's a doormat. It means she's dialed into the long game. She knows that partnership isn't always 50/50; sometimes it's 80/20 with a side of "Lord, fix it before I do."

The Proverbs 31-ish woman does her husband good by choosing grace when she could choose snark. She uplifts him in prayer even when she wants to bury him in laundry. She speaks life when her flesh wants to keep a mental list of everything he forgot, missed, or straight-up did wrong.

But that goodness? It's not fake. It's fierce. It's not just about being "nice." It's about being intentional, wise, and rooted in love that doesn't fluctuate with moods or missed trash pickups.

She's his safe place. His anchor. His "I got you" when the world is throwing punches. She doesn't compete, she completes. Not because she's trying to earn anything, but because she knows who she is and whose she is.

And let's be honest, some days doing him good means tagging him in a meme about weaponized incompetence and still handing him his favorite snack without commentary. That's growth.

Because love isn't always candlelight and grand gestures. Sometimes it's showing up with patience. Sometimes it's choosing silence over sarcasm. Sometimes it's remembering he's God's work in progress too.

So yes, she does him good. And sometimes that good looks like reminding him of the trash schedule taped to the fridge for the third time this month. With a smile. Sort of.

CHAPTER 11: She Works with Willing Hands (And Slightly Bitter Commentary)

You ever fold the same three towels for the fourth time in one day because no one in your house can seem to grasp the concept of "use one and hang it up"? Welcome to the sacred art of working with willing hands, and a little sass on the side.

Proverbs 31 says she works with willing hands. And yes, that sounds poetic and deeply holy. But let's be clear: willing doesn't always mean excited. Sometimes willing looks like showing up to scrub a toilet while having a mental conversation with Jesus that includes the phrase, "Really, Lord? This again?"

She works not because she's desperate for approval, but because she knows the assignment. She shows up for her home, her people, her calling. She puts her hands to the plow, to the laundry, to the Google calendar, to the 1,001 things that keep her world spinning and her coffee reheating.

And she does it all with a kind of grace that's low-key feral. You don't want to mess with a woman in her God-given groove who also hasn't eaten lunch yet.

The Proverbs 31-ish woman knows her work is worship. That wiping countertops and carrying burdens and wiping tears (hers and everyone else's) can all be holy when it's done with heart. She's not looking for applause. She's looking for peace. And maybe five uninterrupted minutes in the bathroom.

Willing hands don't mean she never gets tired. It means she keeps going even when she is. It means she knows when to work hard, when to rest, and when to hand her people a granola bar and go for a walk before she burns the house down.

Her hands are strong. Not just from lifting kids and grocery bags, but from lifting prayers, lifting burdens, lifting others when they don't even realize they're sagging.

So yes, she works with willing hands. And sometimes those hands are doing ten things at once. Sometimes they're flipping pancakes while texting a friend a scripture and unclogging a toilet. But they are faithful hands. Funny hands. Fierce hands.

And when she finally lays them down at night? You best believe heaven sees every single thing they did, even if nobody else remembered to say thank you.

CHAPTER 12: She Is Not Afraid of Snow for Her Household (Because She's Stocked the Snacks and Prayed Over the Pipes)

Snow, in Bible times, was serious business. No salt trucks. No UGG boots. Just cold, danger, and a whole lot of layering. So, when Proverbs 31 says she is not afraid of snow, it's not just about weather, it's about preparedness. It's about being ready when life throws you an unexpected storm.

Now, modern-day snow looks different. It's school cancellations, empty bread aisles, and children suddenly requiring seventeen snacks before noon. But that same principle holds: the Proverbs 31-ish woman doesn't panic, she prepares.

She's the one who knows exactly where the flashlights are and who has a mental inventory of the pantry at all times. Not because she's paranoid, but because she's a planner. And somewhere between prayer and frozen pizza, she's learned how to keep calm and carry a backup generator.

But here's the real flex…her confidence isn't in her checklist. It's in her God. She's not afraid of snow because she knows the One who controls the storm. She's done the work, yes. But more importantly, she's placed her trust. She's wrapped her household in prayer, in peace, in enough toilet paper to survive the apocalypse.

She prepares because she cares. She covers her household in every way; physically, emotionally, spiritually. She knows what each person needs before they even ask. She stocks the snacks, checks the thermostat, and makes sure everyone has a metaphorical and literal sweater.

And even when things go sideways…when the storm hits harder than expected or the power goes out mid-livestream…she doesn't lose it. She laughs. She lights a candle. She serves sandwiches by flashlight and calls it ambiance.

Because fear doesn't run her house, faith does.

So, whether the snow is literal or symbolic, she meets it with grace, grit, and a really good playlist. She is not afraid, not because she's got it all together, but because she knows Who holds it all together.

And if all else fails? She's got a stash of marshmallows and a prayer journal.

CHAPTER 13: She Brings Her Food From Afar (AKA: She Knows the DoorDash Guy by Name)

Now listen, back in the day, bringing food from afar meant hitching up the donkey and heading into town for some wheat, olives, and maybe a goat if it was a good day. It was labor-intensive, dusty, and required serious commitment.

Fast forward to today and let's be real, she still brings food from afar, only now it's via an app. And she does it with one hand while wrangling laundry, a conference call, and a child asking where the tape went (spoiler: it's always in the junk drawer).

The Proverbs 31-ish woman isn't defined by whether she cooked a three-course meal from scratch or microwaved something until it vaguely resembled dinner. She's defined by her heart for serving. Her commitment to making sure her people are fed, even if dinner came from Chick-fil-A and the only thing she "prepared" was the couch. She brings food from afar because she's creative, resourceful, and not above bribing her family with pizza. She knows the magic of crockpots and curbside pickup. She plans meals and also completely forgets to thaw the meat...on the same day.

But what makes her holy isn't the menu. It's the mission. Her food brings comfort, peace, connection. It's less about the calories and more about the care. Her kitchen is her ministry, even if her sink is full of mismatched Tupperware and judgmental spoons.

She's the kind of woman who'll cook a meal for someone in need and send a text to make sure they're eating too. Who brings food and brings herself; fully, intentionally, graciously. Because feeding others is sacred. Whether it's gourmet or graham crackers.

So yes, she brings her food from afar. Sometimes from the freezer aisle. Sometimes from a drive-thru. Sometimes from a deep place of love wrapped in aluminum foil and delivered with a prayer.

And when the DoorDash guy rings the bell, he knows he's not just delivering dinner. He's part of the Proverbs 31 hustle. Tip him well, sis. He's basically family now.

CHAPTER 14: *She Makes Linen Garments and Sells Them (Or Just Opened an Etsy Shop and Can't Find Her Tape Gun)*

Listen, not everyone is out here spinning linen and bartering in the town square like it's a biblical episode of Shark Tank. But the spirit behind this verse? It's entrepreneurial. It's creative. It's a woman using what she's got to build something that blesses others and maybe pays for her Target run.

The Proverbs 31-ish woman sees a need, sees her gifts, and says, "Let's go." She's not waiting for permission or perfection, she's moving with purpose. Whether she's making candles, designing t-shirts, running a side hustle, or organizing neighborhood bake sales with the efficiency of a military operation, she's about that action.

And let's be real: the business life is not glamorous. It's 3 a.m. brainstorming, glitter in places it should never be, and crying in front of Canva because your fonts won't align. It's praying over packages, setting boundaries with clients, and explaining to your kids for the 97th time that "Mommy's working" does not mean "come ask me where your left shoe is."

But she shows up. She markets with integrity. She serves her customers like she's serving the King. Because she is. Her work is worship...even if her receipts are a mess and her "office" is a corner of the dining table covered in snack crumbs and dreams.

She doesn't hustle out of fear. She builds with faith. She knows that what God put in her is valuable. And whether she sells 100 units or just encouraged one heart, she counts it as a win.

So yes, she makes linen garments and sells them. Or she crafts mugs with funny Bible verses, bakes anointed banana bread, or designs planners for women who love Jesus and color coding.

Whatever she's doing, she's doing it like it matters. Because it does. Every click, every creation, every moment of doubt she turns into a declaration.

And if her tape gun is missing? Well, so is everyone's left sock. God is still on the throne.

CHAPTER 15: Strength and Honor Are Her Clothing (But Also Leggings and That One Sweatshirt She's Had Since 2009)

Strength and honor? Yes. And also? That stretched-out sweatshirt with the mysterious bleach stain that somehow became her official house armor. Because while the Bible talks about her clothing like she's draped in dignity, real life often includes mismatched socks and a hope that no one drops by unannounced.

The Proverbs 31-ish woman wears strength and honor not just like a cape, but like a second skin. It's her identity. It's the way she carries herself, not just the clothes on her body.

She's not perfect. But she's consistent. She walks with courage when everything in her wants to curl up and tap out. She speaks with honor even when her kids are testing every nerve God gave her. And yes, sometimes she does it all while wearing a head wrap, yesterday's eyeliner, and the scent of Febreze and holy perseverance.

Her strength isn't loud. It doesn't come with a glittery announcement. It's quiet. Steady. Built in the background while no one's watching. It's holding a hurting friend together when her own heart is breaking. It's leading her home with gentleness and grit. It's facing the unknown and whispering, "God's got me."

And the honor? It's in the way she chooses to show up. In how she doesn't tear down to build herself up. In the way she owns her story…mess and all…and still walks like she's royalty, because she is. She may not feel strong every day. But the strength she wears isn't dependent on her feelings, it's rooted in the truth. And truth looks good on her.

So let them talk. Let them wonder how she does it. She'll smile, adjust her ponytail, and go back to changing the world one load of laundry at a time.

Strength and honor are her clothing, even if her actual outfit says "I've been through something." Because she has.

CHAPTER 16: Her Lamp Does Not Go Out at Night (Because She's Doomscrolling at 1AM)

You ever lie there at 1 a.m., phone glowing like a tiny sun, doomscrolling through social media while promising yourself you'll go to sleep after just *one more* reel? Yeah, same. The Proverbs 31 woman's lamp does not go out at night, but let's just say we've taken that scripture and sprinkled it with modern anxiety and blue light exposure.

Back in the day, her lamp stayed lit because she was productive. She was probably sewing tunics or prepping grain or praying over her household with oil on her hands and a hymn in her heart. Fast forward to today? We're watching cat videos, texting "You up?" to our group chat, and Googling "is it normal to have one leg slightly longer than the other?"

Still, the heart of this verse is about presence. Watchfulness. Dedication. She's not burning the midnight oil just to scroll, she's spiritually lit. She's awake in the dark when others are sleeping because she carries burdens, prays deep prayers, and keeps the home fires burning, even if it's metaphorical and also a little chaotic.

Sometimes her lamp doesn't go out because she's checking on a sick kid. Sometimes it's because she's replaying a hard conversation in her head for the twelfth time. Sometimes it's because she finally has quiet and she's scrolling for memes to cope with the day.

But even in her tiredness, there's a light in her. Not from the phone screen, but from within. A holy glow. A quiet fire. It's fueled by faith, by love, by the relentless pursuit of showing up for her people and herself.

So, if you find yourself awake at night, tossing, scrolling, praying, wondering…know this: your light still matters. Even in the dark. Even when you feel like the only one awake.

Her lamp does not go out at night, not because she's perfect, but because she's present.

And because, apparently, the algorithm thinks she needs to see 14 more reels about decluttering her house before she sleeps.

CHAPTER 18: She Fears the Lord… and Running Into Someone She Went to High School With

The Bible says a woman who fears the Lord is to be praised. And amen to that. But can we also acknowledge the very real fear of bumping into someone from high school while you're in the grocery store, wearing day-three leggings and a look that says, "I gave up during breakfast"? Because same.

The Proverbs 31-ish woman fears the Lord...not in a "lightning bolt is coming" kind of way, but in a reverent, awe-filled, jaw-dropping respect. She knows who He is. She knows His power, His promises, and His presence. And that holy fear is her foundation.

She doesn't serve God because she's scared; she serves Him because she's in love. She worships with her life, her decisions, her "yes" when it would've been easier to ghost the whole situation. She lives with intentionality, knowing the One who holds her accountable also holds her heart.

But let's be honest. The "fear of the Lord" doesn't mean she doesn't have earthly fears too. Like running into Becky-from-Chemistry-turned-Fitness-Coach while holding a frozen pizza and pretending she didn't just detour through the candy aisle. Or remembering that one time in 2003 she wore low-rise jeans and thought it was a good idea.

That's the beauty of grace. God isn't asking her to erase her past...He's inviting her to be transformed by it. To laugh at it. To grow through it. To look back and see how far she's come (preferably in higher-waisted pants and with better judgment).

Her fear of the Lord makes her bold, not brittle. Humble, not hidden. It's the kind of fear that keeps her grounded, steady, and radiant, even when her mascara's melting and she's hiding behind a display of canned corn.

So yes, she fears the Lord. She walks in holy reverence and unshakable purpose.

And if she happens to duck behind her cart when she spots someone from her teenage years? Well, she's still a work in progress.
Sanctified. Sassy. Slightly startled.
But still praiseworthy.

CHAPTER 19: *Charm is Deceptive, Beauty is Fleeting, and Instagram is a Lie*

We've all seen it…those filtered photos that scream "effortless" while hiding a ring light, four apps, and enough editing to make your own mama say, "Is that you?" The Bible says charm is deceptive and beauty is fleeting, and if that's not the most accurate social media commentary ever written, I don't know what is.

The Proverbs 31-ish woman isn't here for the curated nonsense. She knows her worth isn't in likes, angles, or the perfect aesthetic. It's in her spirit. Her character. Her behind-the-scenes love that doesn't always make the grid but makes the kingdom move.

She's not anti-beauty, she's pro-authenticity. She loves a good brow pencil and a Target clearance kimono as much as the next girl, but she also knows that real beauty radiates from the inside. It's in how she listens. How she lifts. How she shows up when no one's clapping.
Charm can woo a room. Beauty can stop traffic. But neither can hold a family together in crisis or pray peace over a chaotic morning.

She's not chasing admiration, she's cultivating depth. That holy kind of beauty that doesn't wrinkle, sag, or expire. The kind that doesn't need a filter because it's been refined by fire.

And on those days when she scrolls and starts to feel small? She puts the phone down, picks up the Word, and reminds herself that her value is not up for internet debate.

So yes, charm is deceptive. Beauty is fleeting. And Instagram? Baby, it's mostly a highlight reel with mood lighting.

But her life? It's the real deal.
Messy. Faithful. Fabulous.
And entirely unfiltered.

The Proverbs 31-ish Woman Rises Again (With Coffee, Christ, and a Hair Tie on Her Wrist)

She's not perfect. Never claimed to be. Her life isn't all fresh bread and folded linens. It's mostly reheated coffee and a to-do list she left in the fridge next to the ketchup. But the Proverbs 31-ish woman? She keeps rising.

She rises when she's tired. She rises when she's doubted. She rises when the world says she's too much or not enough. She rises because the God who called her is faithful…even on days when she's feeling a little feral and a lot forgetful.

She's built something holy in the chaos. Not because she had everything figured out, but because she trusted the One who does. Her strength isn't in her strategy, it's in her surrender.

She's loved deeply. Failed loudly. Prayed messily. And through it all, she's become a walking testimony that grace really does reach the laundry room, the school drop-off line, and the drive-thru window.

This woman? She's every bit as sacred as she is scrappy. She's laughed in the middle of storms, found peace in the pantry, and danced in the kitchen while waiting on a promise.

Her faith isn't perfect, it's persistent. It shows up in texts to friends, sticky notes on mirrors, and whispered prayers over sleeping children. She's proof that you can be holy and hilarious, exhausted and anointed, unsure and still chosen.

And when people look at her life, they may not see flawless. But they'll see fruit. Fruit that fed souls, nourished hearts, and made space at the table.

So yes, she rises again. Not just because she's strong, but because she's held.

And she's not rising alone.

She's rising with an army of women just like her…Proverbs 31-ish and proud of it. Coffee in one hand. Gospel grit in the other. And a hair tie ready to get stuff done.

This isn't the end, darling.

This is just the rising.

About the Author

Diane Ferreira is a Bible teacher, speaker, and author dedicated to equipping women to live out their faith with authenticity, resilience, and joy. With a background in ministry leadership and a deep love for Scripture, she brings biblical truth to life through stories that are both powerful and refreshingly honest.

Known for her relatable teaching style and keen sense of humor, she connects with women from all walks of life, encouraging them to embrace grace over perfection and purpose over performance. Her passion is helping women see God in the everyday and trust Him with everything in between.

When she's not writing or speaking, she's spending time with her husband, Dave, her adult children, and her pushy and spoiled Old English Bulldog.

She believes firmly in the power of prayer, the value of community, and the spiritual gift of good coffee.

You can learn more about her work, speaking engagements, and resources at sheopensherbible.com